thank you, mom!

thank you, mom!
lessons in flowers

by
Heidi Wozniak

**Andrews McMeel
Publishing**

an Andrews McMeel Universal company
Kansas City

www.andrewsmcmeel.com
www.heidiwozniak.com

01 02 03 04 05 LPP 10 9 8 7 6 5 4 3 2 1

Library of Congress Catalog Card Number: 00-109723
ISBN: 0-7407-1425-2

ATTENTION: SCHOOLS AND BUSINESSES Andrews McMeel books are
available at quantity discounts with bulk purchase for education,
business, or sales promotional use. For information, please write to:
Special Sales Department, Andrews McMeel Publishing,
4520 Main Street, Kansas City, Missouri 64111.

for my mom

who made me believe
a scribble was a masterpiece
and a dandelion was a rose.

thank you
for
teaching me
beauty comes in
all ShApEs and sizeS

thank you
for
teaching me
to look at the
BRIGHT side...

thank you
for
teaching me
to trust
my instincts...

thank you for allowing me to nourish my senses

thank you
for
teaching me
the value
of teamwork

thank you
for
giving me
the tools to grow

thank you *for* opening my eyes to the world

thank you
for
giving me
balance
in my life

thank you
for
teaching me
we can *bend*
without breaking

thank you
for
showing me
how to be
gentle yet STRONG

thank you
for
teaching me
to respect
all creatures

thank you
for
teaching me
to appreciate
the sunshine & the rain

thank you
for
teaching me
about honesty

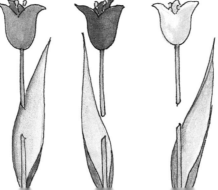

thank you for allowing me to be Creative

thank you
for
teaching me
the value
of hard work

thank you for teaching me life is cyclical

thank you
for
teaching me
a mother's love
is perennial

thank you
mom!
I love you.